Titles by *Langaa* RPCIG

T0198537

K'cracy,
Trees in the Storm & Other Poems

(Composed & Written 1984 – 2006)

By

Bill F. Ndi

Langaa Research & Publishing CIG
Mankon, Bamenda

Publisher:
Langaa RPCIG
(*Langaa* Research & Publishing Common Initiative Group)
P.O. Box 902 Mankon
Bamenda
North West Province
Cameroon
Langaagrp@gmail.com
www.langaapublisher.com

Distributed outside N. America by African Books Collective
orders@africanbookscollective.com
www.africanbookscollective.com

Distributed in N. America by Michigan State University Press
msupress@msu.edu
www.msupress.msu.edu

ISBN:9956-558-74-5

DISCLAIMER
All views expressed in this publication are those of the author and do not necessarily reflect the views of Langaa RPCIG.

To Mami Rubber

Table of Contents

Foreword

This collection would better be rearranged into themes or streams of poetic inspiration! A reflection that has stalled the publication of this anthology. However, I contend that poetic creativity and its inspiration are a drift from the hard and fast rules of algebra, geometry, the laws of physics or arithmetic and trigonometry. The present arrangement has so been done not without the consciousness of the import and need for the lofty idea of structural and thematic unity; but upholding the idea highlighted by scholars of Diasporic Consciousness. On Arguing along similar lines, I would cite a fellow poet and academic, Dr. Mishra who says, "What is peculiar about Diasporic Consciousness is its ability to make connections based on an underground logic of colours, tropes, sounds, texture, moods and secrets. Such association may generate subtle links between seemingly disparate strands and forms." It is in this light that the present arrangement in this volume was made and rightfully picked up by one of the reviewers of this collection who has seen in it "a platter of maze". I consciously refrained from splitting the poems into any sub-categories because the poems themselves like their creator, who through his wondering around the world has keenly observed and followed the paths of political despair, guide the reader through those paths to a Humanist Hope. The individual poems in themselves celebrate, at the same time, a number of human concerns from love, death, birth, innocence, experience, childhood, adulthood, nature and Man to society and politics. How could anyone categorize a poem celebrating love, death, birth and politics? Would it be a political poem, a love poem, an elegy or a nativity poem?

I enjoin you, readers to embrace the poems in this volume not with the idea of finding convenience and contentment but frustration and dissatisfaction engendered by human, social, cultural, economic and linguistic displacements, at home and abroad, which are the driving force behind my message of hope. Being a home and away son, child and poet has provided me the ability to swing to and from and tap from both home and away consciousness leaving my reader with the inner map of this Diasporic Consciousness based on a multiple route logic. Were I to restructure this volume, it would be doing my readers and the volume a disservice.

In guise of a conclusion, I would like to seize this opportunity to thank most especially, those classmates of mine who, in the early days of my writing, spurred me on almost a daily basis to give them something to read and reflect on. I would also like to thank fellow poets like Dr Mishra, Mr Peter Vakunta, Mr Beorn McCarthy, and the novelist, Pr Michael Meehan, scholars who made many useful criticisms of the poems in their manuscript form.

Happy Birthday

❋   ❋

We need no broom!
!Ô   Ô!
We need a darkroom!
Today is a birthday
Not so ordinary a birthday
As it is a rarity of its kind
A day to everyman's mind
One celebrating
The birthing
Of a nation
A nation
With filth
Filled
And for this occasion
Would in a procession
All   march   down
The store with or without gown
And buy a broom
And sweep away our nation's bloom!
Being a wizard neither,
Nor a street sweeper
But one, like all, kept away from uphill
By their broom and briar downhill
Would all with zeal desire
And sweep into the mire
These legends our nation's
Birthing engendered: passions!
Passionate world champion,
Champion of Corruption!

Letter to our deaf father of the nation: "Mr. Dict...."

Let the olive leaves rain!
Let everyone take
His own eyes and feast on you snake
Brook and make
Way for the rain,

Change

Master of mischief and ingratitude!

O, Mr. D...!
You think your life thorny,
For we dare think,
Speak,
Write and act... songs
To right your wrongs!

O, Mr. D... every hour
With adoration we greet your
Gallows popping up in the manner
Of mushrooms
At every street corner
With zeal hungering for us like grooms

Their brides,

And we ask for no doom
But our rights,
Our birth rights!

And quest if you're a mushroom
Eating champion
To scheme such reprobation
As never did any power trickster
Even to his own hamster!

You erect in our country
Such gallows as the tallest tree
Would never match
And on which our rights are bashed

Diurnal and nocturnal!

We having just one never to end a journal!

Seeing you harpoon all those rights,
Those of our republic,
Those of your republic,
Those even defined by others
As being human;
And even our birth right
To live,
  Love,
    Think,
      Speak,
        write,
Act
  And
    Die
  Freely
Just as   you   live
  And
  Will   die   live
(And Miserably
       Too!)
Thank and thank your god
We have heads and will not
Help, help you
Abridge your affliction
Pushing us into the heights of tribulation….!

Nudging you to the head
We thought you had a head
We thought you knew what rights
Were ours
And which were yours…!
Foreseeing no plights,
We thought the bright gaze
On your face
[A new page!]
Replicated some goodness
In you concealed!
We now know your head as empty
As the bellies of our fellow human beings
'Littering' your streets
& wanting in food and water;
We know it emptier
Than the calabash of that
Desert Wanderer whose thirst
Harried him to you

And you ushered him
To the garrotte chamber!
Breaching the Contract!

Knowing that shimmering seal's
Face, the rot in you conceals
We would…
Not in the woods…
Hoot you down!

Step down, renege the crown
To hap your way under
As we
With our thorny
Life of misery …

Do!

Do, bury your mulishness!

A Song For African Heroes
(Lost in the War Against AIDS & Associates)

Oh! Men of Africa,
Oh! Men of the cradle to humanity
Lost in this War
You must be true and bold as warriors be

Oh! The blessed memory!
The blessed memory
Of the days death and dying
Were far removed and remote from our thinking…!

Oh! Today, Today!
As part of you Men and children of Africa though not home this day
I cannot but greet your courage;
The courage with which you feed this killer sneer in a rampage!

Just as I do applaud your grit
So do your death and dying my ears greet
To aggrieve grieving souls
Grieving the departed souls!

Bewildered, I quest the associates of Mr. Killer
And through my mind flashes poverty
But I doubt seeing the ocean of wealth in which swims Africa the Beauty!
And I start thinking of Mr. Seducer!

Still, no answer but only hope for the souls of the departed
Faithful or not, to Rest In Peace
All those kids full of hopes and thoughts of great deeds now departed
I knew them harbouring no thought or dread of death; they're at ease!

The Ease, oh! The Ease they were at!
The Hopes, oh! The Hopes they had!
The thoughts, oh! The thoughts they cherished!
Ease, Hopes and Thoughts all in the grave dashed!

And even mine, yours and theirs
Would have gone with them to the grave
Leaving family, friends, you and I
In Black despair were we not all grave!

Oh Heroes! your loss is but a battle
And as long as a soul lives on shall continue the battle
For the war to be won

With lives being the price for this to be done!

Heroes, rest in Peace !
And remember the Ease!

None saw them coming,
They marched in draping Africa
With such bleak and sombre shadows
Of the starless night
Trapping true sons and daughters of the soil in the lightless light
And trapping you in a battle to defend your kingdom
Like knights of old their kingdom

Hearing the Voiceless

In spite of this gripping quiet and blackness surrounding,
This special melodic, rhythmical sound emerging from within
Defies human description and scrutiny
And hints on the overwhelming importance
The overwhelming importance
Of the connection
The connection
Of the Inner Voice
And the voiceless, their voice
Within telling their travail,
Hopes and aspirations shall prevail
In the like this melody is savoured
And thankfully hearing this sound I am favoured!

Seeing From The Other Side

Poverty is the rich man's nightmare
Richness is the poor man's dream
One colourful dream
None can spare
And all would bear

The thoughts of poverty ware
The rich
And same enrich
The poor
Drive them to industry
As it does the rich to misery

And why not the third world's?

The Wealth Of Poverty

I smile where others will cry
I laugh where others will moan
I need just a meal a day
And this is where others need three

I content myself with the pangs of hunger;
My daily lot
Just as others
With this hurry to the doctor's,
For the slightest feel of it
And I am so friends with stress
that I seem not to see
And feel that ogress
Sending many a thousand to the psych...

The slightest loss I know its impact,
And knowing what it means to lose the little you did sweat to get....
And here others will scuff at its smallness
And I tell 'em what matters is littleness
Through which I sec life's fineness
Compounded finely

Beyond Sentient Patience

Like the strings of a harp
Accord and make no catalogue
No catalogue of mishap
        With one misery in a miserable monologue….
          Whether or not the wind blows
        Just go on and receive the blows
Of misfortune
That's out of tune
Smashing
     'n Crushing
     The defiant
        Giant….
And on you falling
Like those on a harp string!
Take no break
Apply no brake
Don't cry
On the spot, fly….
Not away
It is the only way
     And that
And only that
From Providence frees man
     And from the human!

Thirst: Would Our Heads Understand

Stage the biggest war
Create the supreme fight
To show your might
And in the name of fame
And I will tell you all is the same
For me: an awe!

Greatness does not come by war
Greatness never passes through a door
He dwells inside
And shows the light....

People struggle to be great
Great to the world by grade(s)
And none seeks him inside
The grave nor by its side!

Greatness once was
Greatness now is
Greatness shall be
That which has always been;

Graciously gratefully great
And peacefully inward
Marching toward no ward
And seeking not even a groat...!

The Racist Black
(A Prose for the Headless African[1])

An African,
A Princely African
Proud to bee
And letting no nonsense bee….
Promenading in Paris
By the pub door sees

A gorilla-like Black male
Like one ready for blackmail
In his gibber, he bars the door to a Black
"To night, the pub is all women,"
Yet, letting in White men…!

And the Prince is all green in the dark…!

---

[1] This poem in prose might never be read by any of those conscienceless African security guards posted in front of such place as the one here described nor by those who place them there…! But, there is hope that one day their offspring might be schooled enough to understand the significance of the colourlessness of "Black & White" in Fine Arts…!

Presence

Foretells absence
Once foretold
And defined in the old
Without her;
Why dread her?

Just a child
I grew wild
Calmed my mind
Though in a bind
And decided to settle
Of course not in a kettle
So, I dreamt of a swallow
And was swallowed
Everywhere I went
And quested not what it meant
And   today by a   bird
Swallowed I dream of a bed
In which to rest
For that's my nest
And for sure
I'll take pleasure
Being swallowed in there
Especially by my honey mer-
Maid for whom I travel
And for love   I travel….
She came for love
She came
And together we shall come
And derive great joy of calm
For I know the hearts beat
On either side: beat
Not for fear
But for they come near
And Me in the bird fly,
Heed no fly!

Freedom Givers
(In Old Dahomey)

We are the Da Suzas
Proud as never one was
To have freed negroes
Freeing them to bondage
Paving their one way voyage
And witnessing the family coffer grows!

How else can you style Us?
For sure not pus…!

Sweet Exile

All on our way home,
                    One day
Like our ancestors
Hunter gatherers
We migrated to clean up
                    And build up
                                    Their cities of today
And in hope to go home,
            Go home with the gathered game
And still we return maimed,
                        Thirsting for fame
As centuries went by leaving all the same…!

Glen

Down by the rue de Dunkerque
I met an Irishman by name Glen
He had a girlfriend by name Sharon
And as we bade one another, "Hello!"
I thought of the hell hole
The one from which they hail.
As I probed further
He in a rage screamed:
"You can't understand
Being African the problem is Irish
And you can't understand anything ANC…"
I laughed
At the remembrance
Of those days as a schoolboy
When scanning

                "An Irishman Foresees his death"
                "The Bloody Sunday"

And playing Singe's "Show-boy…"
And a host of others
Were all with my world one!
How could I know anything about this
And being all else but Catholic,
And having been everywhere else safe in Ireland
And in prison
Lord safe my soul
He waxed his ears for four miserable years
In prison spent
And I wonder if every Irish

                Brigand
In   Prison
Be hailed Hero …!

Ridding

Canker worm
Supersedes
World's martyrs
Causing no regretting
With no sense of belonging
To a crèche….
Though human
And
Humane.
                                But
          Reveries
Victor's Driver
Takes one through.

Hostages

Prison wall
Mocks all.
Libidos like pirates
Hunting hostages
Ravishes them,
Drives them in
To leaving in
Smear-like
Tadpoles
Hosted in aura's poles
In which caught,
Wiggle worm-like
Shoots
Skating around aura,
Humming freedom
In tombs hidden,
Reached through doom
When in bird-like cages,
But, deaf, dumb and blind
All on reserve bench
With panegyric under
Phear's aegis
Hail'em
Great men
Hoping this passage
From bondage
Frees them
For freedom wall
Falls to free all.

Another Messiah Is Born

The circle pregnant with V
On V Day eve
At polls' maternity
Did unbundled her womb's content.
The French have chosen from J,
And alphabetically too....!

                                  Date, Seventh May.

Today, like Chaucer's May,
A tiny rain droplet
In the ocean landed. I observed
This lonesome spectator swim,
Swimming in the ocean of men
Who like fishes, at the Concorde,
Discordances' legacy
Where our new born Messiah
Will of contention apple taste
Hailed with contentment
May's birth
And gender and gender alone
Marks Chaucer's, not the psyche!

Our droplet in the ocean with keenness
Listened to cries of joy hailing
The turning of a new page
A new page at every age
                                  Turned
How many so far turned?
How many so far unturned?
These questions, I saw in him, like smoke rose.

The fitment gilded
Like grand father's grave grange
Graced with promises of employment,
Would-be deployment,
Greased this easy birth.

Outsiders needn't meddle in kitchen politics.
I would he could
Air out that thought and be heard;
Still a stranger in the maze
He chose but gaze !

Christ turned water into wine.

My new Messiah,
Former Hate of State,
Newly born head of State
At birth conjured
Apple trees sprouting
And fruit bearing
At every street corner
On building walls
And everywhere at the Concorde
To help water displacement
Provoked by the human ocean!
He is change!

Time! Midnight.
Pensively homeward making
Stares at would-be loafers,
Apple eaters;
I heard him laugh out
And voice: "Chaucer,
Come, come thee and witness May
Today, this May day.
'45, '95. Loathsome mayday!"
and like heated vapour
he evaporated from the crowd; crying: "the poor
I wish new Messiah's promises
Outlived Daffodils !"

With him d'accord,
I pondered still, if the ejected *J*
Was not also a *V*
In the circle, incubated.
And Change what change
Shall thou bring messiah?
I too must quit
For his acclaim's worth is sh…t !

From the Whitehouse to the Kremlin
From Westminster to Berlin
And today the Elysée once welcomed a Messiah
And all had a desire….

Remains: New Arms Stardom

Arms rumble and crackle fire
Spitting in your inner C.Ts.
Harvesting minds not artificially sown
And like sea waves
All day, day long,
Your ship, life, unend staggers
'twixt Queens and Harlem;
Royal Palaces for Pavrety,
So the other side of dear
                              Manhattan
Gentrifying you two gear city.
Manhattan above in heaven
Like a mount in the horizon
Licks the ar…, heaven's
Really Golden Boys Haven,
Your Queens under in abysm,
Solid foundation for mount Attan
Your weight stand
And on two speed
Waddles life in the coffin,
Old New Amsterdam's

Forest Guile

It looks dangerous
Penetrating her by night
Scaring like the most delicate
Person, one disease afflicted
With the gloom of the darkest night;
But, she is free
And her joys sparkling
Than the brightest sunny day;
For her health is ascertained.
                'Tis by day,

                        Mosquitoes
                Scorpions
                 Snakes…

        Infest
        Forest
And by night to prey,
Free   her
How then by night
Is the forest
Not a refuge, safest?

In my herd

The one cattle standing
As the greatest menace,
Through docility, wanting
                              Grandeur...
Getting her on knees
                    Simple:
                              Milk her
To becoming
                    Wan   having
In her
The   World's
G
      R
            E
                  A
                        T
                              E
                                    S
D   E   S   E   R   T
                                          For
                                          My

            ALIBI.

White
Paper sheet
As you gave opaque pen
One kiss
Worse than
Night
Fall
Your plain's defined
None dreams a grain
Nor loss again
Impregnated ye carry
Words
To turn out
Machine gun-like, pout
Horror for Head
And
Lullaby for the un
I beam with joy
Like a loving guy
Who gleams his gun
To the head pointed;
With them brush in hand
To painting
The guy subversive king.

A Century Ago

Each time a child is born
Parents fire gun
Hoisting total joy
Especially when he is a boy.
I saw them throng
Our dome for the baby I was; strong.
All that came were sane
None insane
And none a saint
But amongst them, one, quaint.
At my sight
He sighed;
I saw questions dancing
On his mind for my coming;
One quested mundane weirdness,
Another life's senselessness.
With a lively smile
Unbeguiled
I told my baby self
Never to pave way to this elf
'Cause 'twas meaningless
venturing to coin any from the senseless.
There at work is nature
Inscribed in the proverbs of the scripture....

May Be In A Dream

I don't think
I don't drink
Just about to pen opposites
Whence Walcott hurtled in with "Negatives"
I stammered
With his voicing in them hit – la!
He and him are down in History
And we have at least a story;
The one in the military
The other in the literary
And I bow to the literate,
His militancy not the military illiterate
Against literacy
Driving him with arms crazy
Giving an amount of nous
To name them …. God knows!
Both militate
One destroys, the other creates.

The Seine By Night
[*A Regular Visitor P(un)der(s)*]

Plodding down
Pondering dawn,
Halt or glide smoothly
Leaving the homeless lonely?
Oh, Liberty!
Sweet liberty!
Were you not Faustus'
Queen in parade
Magicking away in raid
In maze letting us
No, the profane
Would, France had another fame
And she is your country
Country of Liberty
And to you married
When she in her have you buried
And I see you in parade
Like the French military in parade
To give true meaning to come
To that which you have become
And I continue my song
When liberty is unsung
        Oh,   Freedom
                 Freedom
                 Freedom
        Oh,   Freedom fighters
May you be born again for us
To have eighty-nine more years
And sing thy sweet name
With all the joys and no pain
And be glad you live Liberty!

                      And that you are not a scarce commodity!

Platitudesmaybe

Did we learn history?
Is nothing, nothing?
Nothing is nothing!
We are
US
WHY?
Something
To be
In
Which
All nothing see
And like clouds'
Story told…
They passed
No doubt
Above us
And we set
Pace for a world
That is
Ifanyis
And
To be
And
Paltitudesmaybenought.

Stained Garb

Early morn, it is.
Up, pick I the coat.
Dismal it is.
Dreamt I of a moat.
And a knock at its post
Lay my pump lamed
Blood though it pumped,
Jejune is the coat.

The Inner Being

Perching all day long
Wondering that's becoming of man,
A word makes its précis,
Westwardness, yet for others the reverse
And as news of inventions reach us;
We applaud for the illusions.
Uncaged instantaneously,
The wonders are for extermination;
Nucleus of the children
Hiroshima and Nagasaki.
Today, germs of the long forgotten
Excavates. We dream
Of gold, perishing our mind
The way the world ends!

To The Jap

You say I am Black,
Yes! I am Black!
Not as you paint me.
I take the moon's bright and you the sun's,
Refuting glory from me once came;
And that at the apogee of mine
Yours its commencement saw.
You shall crash and slump
Then will I stand.
Do that which you are doing?
Or just that you tell me…?
He was not a dunce
Modeling a spherical surface for us
'That you ignore!
'Tis a pity you're not that you claim!

As Sun Sets East

With head up
Posted alone
In a chalice only
Canst thou
A company eye
Though
The great William
Shook his spear
Stimulating our larynx
Like would a sphinx
To vibrating
Songs and thinking
A cup is here provoking
Bestial desire
While snatching the desired
Might for its consummation,
This reflection
Mirrors Edutilos
Whose uniqueness
West imprints
Feminine revolutionary keys:
L. E. F.
As Frank as Gaullists
Whose the Gaulle
Fathered
Kindred
From the globe part
Obscured, with no light
Igniting lachrymal glands'
Summer as he saw
His box at park
With no alternative
But journey along stiff,
For it is full with age,
Period! He goes in a cage!
'Tis history
We hear the story !

A Fisherman Dreams

By the river Nun I stand
My hooks I have in hand!
In writing, question markers
They are. In rivers
Question fishes:
"Why- waste time here?"
Inciting them: "Follow us home in a creel,
Bask yourself upon the hearth,
Fill our father's
Bowels
And his senses abduct
As you question
Your stay
And say:
'Farewell
Bowel !'"

Come's The Time

For the cur all along we wait.
For its tykes long we never as bait.
Of ruggedness is the 'scape's face.
Yet, we it still embrace.
But, come is the time.
Lulling its forward march?
No way? To let it, we must slump then.
Put on our last putrid rags.
Jolly are some, chanting and dancing.
Others, left and right stolid heads, tilt.
Heads' stolidity for missing.
For with gold they could this hinder.
For never is this not impossible;
While for mouths and stomachs those dance....

Wreck

At storms' wheel
Mast underlooking water
At will
On knees goes to kiss her;
Sinks obligated
With captain subjugated
Like gloom of factitious light
Under sunlight
With the bayonets facing death
To embrace it, one day, in dearth.

Instinct

You fast illusive, silly and idiotic fellow,
Why make you people misbehave?
Seriously distort you people's mind;
Won't let soundly sleep them;
Because they are driven blind.

Why haunt you not Utopia?
Ought you inhabit uninhabited homes.
Be me for ever happy with thy cleavage.
Unbearable repulsive ailment, can you
Be cured? If …. How? Why not?

Nature be divine, yes!
Thou play thy part, make idiots
Bold and dreadless of no nonsense;
To wise men, dreadful of nonsense.
Tell me thine cure, me bid thee adieu!
For ever.

We Preys

From a hole, whole!

With a friend, coming
Coming into a parlour, we got in.
He the bedroom could sense be good.
I had yet felt it could.
Tall, up in the air, he stood.
Short I was seated on a stool.
To the next we made our
Furrow a perch. In the heart
Of that cabin I pondered, and felt
The cadavers we in it left:
Condiments needed by the glutton;
Refuted he, he shall the glutton feed
But, mittens have our gloves been.

When the clocks were set at work, they began,
Winding up were the climbers
Now embracing a stoop
At this point, the spears cast afar.
To identify where came the spears' end,
Many moon phases it took my friend.
Nowhere, but tipped nostrils.
Though crawling, distinguished I many faces
In the moon; scraped him the sky yet made none.

Still his clock was at naught.
A blank sheet knows ink when written on.
Out of use it runs when, by the scribe, filled,
The scribe, cook number one, sets it
And to the door post keep
For our unheard of friend to gloat,
And place its inevitable cold hands.

The forest in which stand, these houses
Never had we gone in. Never!!
Nor did we the biggest forest tree discover.
Yet, the scribe cannot manufacture
It to feed on itself
As soil after storm to itself return
Dust particles we are, to soil return?
Why come through the travails of pools
And to soil return, not pools?
And without soul whole lodge we in holes.

Fools Themselves

Cartels   Nourishments

In Human   Psyche

Egg Barons   And   tycoons

Toddling   IN   Bleak Bright Blackness

With their

Shackles

Chain

Serfs

In

New Haven   for   Blackpools'

The   Grime,   from   Baronlessness

Ailing   To   Tycoonlessness

To pivot societal four walls

On their sinking sands Barons

And tycoons

Themselves   Fool

As

In

Chains   Serfs

With ease, in storm, espouse

New   Vanes

In   Mist

To unscreen   Sunshine East

Erecting   tenacious   card   castles

Nor   storms nor   waves budge a little

Circumvented   Barons

Preventing waffles flying   to serfs

Fool   only   themselves!

Our Lot

Festive merriment in youths
Under the clouds beyond the bounds
Models nature; embraced like man
With only the river fed by man,
His tears. The hopeless lights reflect,
Mapping his cause's defect.

Hurdles

Light invisible on it, eye we;
The fine ray stream, shines dark:

For never is the followed brightness seen,
Above, the bright sun is black,
At dawn, to the east no ray,
Yet when to the west taken is the head,
Darkness is the ray.
On this spot, together seems to come;
The globe that never has come.
The skies, rising from the ground.
Yet beneath sinks all the ground.
From the earth's four walls,
Proceeds the journey; the coming earth,
But, Arêtes and Pyramidal Peaks
The calories sap, and the quarries,
To the mire them drown,
Up to the large moon, look we
Yet, identify we but a star.

Rain Dance
(Daunting)

fateful
seasons
embrace
tropics'
dryness
rains' Reigns
      As
Rats gulp music
      In
Flood goading
Their heads'
Swine Greed
These tyrants
Steel hemmed
Daunt skunks…!

Pari(S)Ah

I dream of a country
In whose bottom ye
Crushed were buried....

Bleak city heart so bright
Outward villas at night
In the village rifts
Towers of the vilest streets
Thine eyes on this Earth's scum
Tempt for ye honour
Walk's invitation
Already in the streets
Trailing along bags
On backs no way back
We started shouldering
         Trash
        We're
T' mark twilights' dawn west

I dream of such Queendom
For this world here's their kingdom
Habouring Pari(s)ahs
All day and night knights
Mustering brighter might
In the villas 'bove
Towering them muzzles
Bubbling inward with
Larvae to bring villas
Down their heels in slumps
Toning mutiny
Glorious festival
So long awaited
And now on Joy's altar
For vicissitudes
Sweeping demagogues
Standing pedagogues
To teach one lesson
Just one 'I shall. If...'
With the break of Eve's
Day 'I shall' is slain
Leaving companion
For our feast's seeds' yeast....

We've rid the weeds

Giving new dawn life
And we host still plight
Willing this wavering
Dawn our smiles broadens
As we queue in files
With angst marking time
To pursue this line
March forward against
Any reversal
'Cause they'd counter-rival
With intent to gallows
Preserve our kind low
At the peak period
To which we mark period
Seeing the crown down
Lackeys shall frown
To down the Roy
We'll not but Joy.

Paris : Is It?

An interesting experience
Mirroring my youthful days
When sheepishness pushed me in the heart,
The heart of a desert, so deserted
That not even a date was in sight
Turning all one possessed as vision,
A weird wide world to come
A dream come reality,
Thought, then real fiction
Constituting the funniest of all fun
From a clown whose only wisdom
Resided in the clattering of the ribs of his entourage
At all stages.

Today's greatest desire is : give
To those thinking my kind naïve
That illusion
Making 'em lose their brains
Having a laugh, saying :
"This fool is the worst sand grain,
On him one cannot build."
But the duty of a clown?
Create your dependence
On his acts for your lungs' health.
And doing this consciously
For the clown is lively
'Cause it be strange,
In these dying days of our age,
Replica of reason's age
Having difficulties spotting "Idiots" hidden prime role;
Desiring to test
The wisdom of the wise.

The thought of the masses
Nowhere constitutes a balance sheet
Of universal wisdom and truth
Though one in this lot discarded
Idiot may hold the truth.

Our Kind Stepmother

O, what! A heaven?
My old lad to the market went
Amongst the jumble lasses,
Cocoyam leaves of all chose he.
Yet, knew not him of it;
Docility breeds passion and badger,
Dumbness is viper's co-author
To paint clothed dragon

For the chattel, he thrice paid
To the natural uncapping,
Dangling was his head, this way and that....
His wrinkle surface face undulation coal painted
Testify he never a scorpion
Anywhere bought to sting communion.
Wailing, are we with joys heading
Hands looking only west.

The crocodile eye keep on her eggs.
Smashed must be those neighbours
Smashing them. She then dunces hatch,
Snatching the shark-to-be's ability
For him never to his silhouette cut.
Yet, to its summit, his wraith would an image raise.
Sabbaths keeps the dragon and services performs.
Why should this serpent glance at verses,
Not coming up with unsoothing analyses?

Cartridges

Papers' filigrees
From my nip trickling
Hail filibuster;
Were silence golden
To sleep sea would
                      Plop
Words cajoling ears,
Caressing hearts,
              Embroidering desires'
     Quest
  To ignite conquest….
Bleeding from black over white.

All In A Second

Postulating our worlds round,
For three six weeks lying unbundled
Screams and squeaks drop the bundle
To relieve gestation burden
As the bundle break open
Bringing forth life,
Pushing it towards the grave,
Bridge to the hereafter,
Questing Grace
And back to the then after
Instantly sums life;
The Bright?

The Blacks' Blight

My Prayer

Oh God!
May my appellation tempt thee
Show mankind the light
Not through a Being
Likely to breed Thomas
But through the light
That like sun shines
'Cos tiredness of embracing nights'
Chill in broad daylight
Is on my table

Over-demanding is revolting
Seeking equality
Thou deemst still reverse
Ultimate
But give the devil his due
Knower of all with a design
Thou bred him
And must his thirst quench
For the fire by which
Thou sat him
Flashes the light of this world

God
Let all your own light
See and not for a fragment shine bright
Amen.

Sunset

My boyhood's gone
From dust, away, blown,
Blood of cities
To impose on me homeless grits
My progress outward
Others watch that which I saw
With old god's needles nailed,
In the darkest room concealed
For being adversary
Would or not, stand
Rain of taint
From the West taking its rise
To receive no grain of rice
                              At

Sunrise.

U – Suffrage

To the celestial,
A concept so alien
We the terrestrial
Hold fast to, exponent,
Gusting societal doctrine
East, towards western latrine
Feeding nasal
Senses on pungent capital
Stint Like Edgewood
Defensemen taking descend;
All is demo-crazy!

Pyramid,
Top of celestial,
No vote or self vote,
It is d'accord
To the terrestrial
Like desert storms
Raise clouds....
Clouds of dust....
Dictatorship, book-keeper
Of celestial wisdom
And defendant of earthly kingdom,
Demo-crazy makes his driver.

Vain Glory

Child of Steps towards equation
Who images life one for all
Blurring odds 'twixt men
And with the greenest eyes drinking
Others for they eject dejectedly
Thoughts of supremacy
Denuding this to those in her garbed
To over-fall in a bottomless pit
Ideal grave for Vain Glory....

Complex "S"

Man's supremacy,
His tendency
To thinking
In our world were
Idiots as the odd ware
Whose brains deadened
By their ability to drinking
Defined it fine
And could not find,
Not even a smile
In the squareness
Of the mess
Thought voiced,
Never heard,
Not even after a head
Like Thautin Tom's
Worked out the sums.

The Transfer

Upstairs comes the demand
Downstairs is the job manned
The transfer from one building
Face to face they are standing
In the swamp's building, gauges
The hide-brimmed-furry mountain luggage;
In the swamp farm, it then the fertilizer scatter....
As if wind weaned, and short of water
The sturdy luggage the room chokes
Then the room quits, sapped
While swamp's room's woolen outside carpet door
After ampere shocks, keeps open door.

The Scum

When ecstatic, dogs wag
In garbs men brag
Ignoring and depriving dog's joy
Cutting tail off these guys
Reading in them heartless masters
Sowing their disasters.
Like God working Satan's

The Greyhound

all young dogs
are the type one would eye
with great awe
that with which our
lads, the barons wont
gladly glimpse
at with joy instanta as is
the case with my hound
who at the sight may grind
not but bone
all alone

he is short
  loves the master's
   his gaits as he makes
      even the shortest of the short
        ever in history of man known
it is this you get
about my lying dog at the gate

The Gospel

Of all God's servants
The most obedient is Satan,
Most favourite, man
Ignites in him, bilious green
To hauling up His Master
For partiality,
Negating the Word, Master's
And on the Bench, would weight
Master Right
Like a poet, painter, architect,
Creating life
For critics dual admiration
Not changing the created structure;
Most obedient Satan's advocacy.

American Dream Village

Far from being
Hell where for living
Devine intervention
From human gods
Sing indispensability
She is fractioned
And displayed
Like a casket
Of Gold
And a basket
Of mould
This western Rose blossoms
Beckoning eyes to her bosom
To feast on the golden casket,
Just a glacial basket
And her being on heat
Embraces shriek
Projecting coins' other side
With freedom's flag
Each American eye
Would it passed by.

Tryst

God in his humble
Intents did stumble
He fashion the face
Of the earth with lace
Tinted with colours
White and black emitting dolour
Leaving the one saint
And the latter stained;
All he does brings behind
'M critics to grind,
Grinding to awakening
His scope; he's the scum and nothing,
And I think the omniscient
Too blind
Leaving reflections
On equality notion
Sprouting from political trees,
Just like in academic fields
Where the God-created lovers
Meet to project intimacy
Which never was, but hypocrisy
As the one must mount
On the other to pound,
Crush his world.
This is our world
And our tryst is told
With the rumble of a bolt.

Our Bride

There she stood
                                                            Like a bride
                                                                    Awaiting a groom
                                                        At the thought of whom
I heard the church bell ring
                            Stealing me away from my thinking
                                    To tilting my head
                            To the Church door step
                    And feast my eyes on that colourful wreath
Whose flashing bright light
Projects some   light
                                        Years
In to this future
                                                        At which a blend of ecstasy
                                            And a ghostly chill dribble down my spine
                            Brought by none but the gloom
                                                        That in the church looms
With the echoes of the priest's
                                    Resounding voice
Bringing home   a prayer for   the departed
Faithful
                                Or unfaithful,
            Martyr   or   Hangman
And I would I were a best-man
                    Seeing someone has just passed   Away
So much as to avoid our Bride
The one to whom   we shall all be tied
                            I paused:
My turn awaits
                    Me
            Someday
                And I wonder whether the bouquet's flashy colours
                        Of pink, red, blue, and white roses
                        Shall constitute the beauty to grace
                        My departure from a World so
                            Turned down side up
                        Re-plunging me into that pensiveness
                            To pick up a pen
                            And pen
                            The anxiousness
                            With Which all wait...

My Happy Plight

Look, look
Look at
      me
Poor
        me
                                                      Here I am

Here in
The
      Wilderness
This asylum
        Wherein   blossoms
Blindness visible to the blind
Poor, poor
        me
With my sight
From all fight
                                        I stay
                                        Away

              Out of reach
                 From the blind Rich
And like a beam
              Craving that day
My ears that treasure away
      Steal
That loving prattling
          Of jays
And even that loathed thundering
Applause of the crackling canons at a battle
Applauding the colourless blind
Colour blinding
           The Rich with their colours
Only to them visible
Thought by the world
           Sightless
For they live off a bottle…
           My eyes let them flow…!

K'CRACY.

                                                        Ah! Then, a shepherd,
                And now, a farmer.
                                                How dubious was the shepherd?
How faithful is this new comer?

            The Shepherd's herd mealed unappetizingly
                But hoped having appetite.
            Tyrannically, he them lead peacefully.
            Could not this be debunked in time?

Submissive was herd during his reign,
Though an Anarchist was this K'crat.
Not until after that first K'cratic reign;
Fanatics of that reign never turned mad.

Revealed now, he has been,
                                Must trial stand;
To be imprisoned, found he had been
"Unfair trail' this judgment he termed.

Once worshiped as God herdsman,
Now lead painted caricature and "obstinate' term,
                                Though like gold he once glittered
Deserves harshness from his one time State.

Our obdurate farmer seems faithful.
And sceptical policies he introduces
Yet, not all that is he unvengeful
Unravelled would be that after he dies.

Blind we were not to an intelligentsia see and choose
For others loaves were buttered
For they saw and chose
Ours never was and never will be buttered.

But this farmer cares less for his plants
The shepherd's incarnate proves-he
Yet, to the plants,
Much for their "good state' cares-he.

So droopily carry 'em smiles
For their yearnings winning
But homily carry herd and plants smiles
For they longed not for the K'crats craving

The Shoots

In the dusty season he to the valley took'em,
Knee crooking, "Sir" he the herdsman answered
At the height of his glory, he him chased;
Coal painting him, and yet, has he the genotype.
In the cave the skeleton they keep to the card mastermind
And diurnal unknown destination travel we hear announced.

The change that ever place took
Never was anymore than night followed by
An eclipse profounder than night.
And replaced Mask
Though nightly painted is cleaner
For the darker genotype is the cleaner phenotype.

The Versatiles

Of the same gang was he!
At medical detachment pronouncement,
More than anybody was he nostalgic;
Though not to the tune dance but to pilot our ship.
Avoiding to dance to the tune of herdsmen,
His predecessor him loved; would he forget?

More than this new band leader,
The spurious wholesaler ever we saw
Under four squeamish manufacturers
Our ship an outboard motor made
To be extolled with a sinecure.
On our knees forced we him and his House hear say "No!"

Behind our backs curse them Us
Never is he not unwilling to let any,
No matter whom but his embryo him replace.
Once to this experiment put,
Than the best ever tried, a card castle,
As was in storm crumbled not infant's breath.

Yet, the exposed unclothed intransigence
Socketed than ever, fused'em:
The Herdsman, the Wholesaler and this Leader.
For their sake millions their clocks at bay kept.
Leaving no third, in his father's stomach gold plants,
Parsimoniously garbles the child than father....
Never in front of our retina, all these !

Family Feud

We enjoy the wind
When she blows in a hot, hot day
And good news come promising
Freshening atmosphere...

Our father sits in
Would not with us enjoy her
'cause he would rather sniff
and force us to take hot indoor air.

We as prisoners
Seeking escape sneaked out
As he took to his chambers;
came to the parlour while we're out,

he hate this fresh air
and loves French air
enjoyable only abroad,
not this waste intoxicated one aboard

our one real father
has children at heart
depriving them of fresh air
his prerogatives found abroad

impairing everything
his ego echoes to him
not to heed our plight
for it shall make us bright

father is good
and drinks out of a gourd;
the family's, alone
constantly getting loans;

viewing us trees
with many branches
carried by a trunk
and wishing we were not styptic strong

and under the loan
weight we only groan
as he beams with a smile
to style

us: family brigands
desiring his bones

as we, to challenge
him, ask for change
insults on us coil
and we look onto ancestral soil

we can't be prisoners
where freedom is ours
a birth right
not a privilege of life….
as if fall is not his and his entourage,
their incumbency mirrors
shrubs' question to trees
uprooted by wind.

but like all other stems
ours beacon a season
to conduce stun them
with cutworms,

plants' predators
who'd not pray for trees
as would for the younger or stunted
wrinkled fatherlike shrubs….

preys and predators
must not like alligators
and lizards, say: "well done"
not dream of a by-gone;

predators' have preys
mandate and must not scare preys
like our father has us
and would not bury scaring us

projecting himself as palm fronds
refusing the twigs the embrace of wind;
fighting her from reaching them
when she blows hard.

Stale-Word (Hope)

Hopelessly hopefully optimistic.
Accidents occur, I was told.
And in a contest, to me occurred.
Yet, I came back; alive!
Then saw I the wrong of the world,
Though right I have been thinking it.
'Tis happened,
Should one 'cause of trifle
The ghost give up?
Life goes on after all!
But hope I love more
Is one to be hated more
That it works against our wish
Hope not for this type: the squeamish,
For it sharpens pains
Hoping against hope,
A stale word: hope
Hopeless like desert plains.
In those long gone days
Adulthood I thought nice;
Now for my childhood I long
For it is better stay in dark;
We in ignorance
See everything bliss,
Than live in light that is bleak,
Unable to effect change
'Cause of the thousand bayonets
screening the pavements
those leading to the doors of change.
Squalid Hope!
As a child, under trees
I watch the demotic leaves
Already transformed from green to brown,
As the fall off trees....
Enchanted one is
Thinking of the replacing leaves
To take a different green and shape;
Yet, all from the former they take
And when wind blows,
The fallen leaves laugh,
Laughing at their successors
Draining from root through stems
Into none but themselves
For they are no better!

Yet, I hoped for vicissitude….
Laughed at by fallen leaves!
Puerile, horrid Hope!
However the journey I started,
Realising the 'scape full of ruggedness,
Still all was hope to go through
Red carpet
Wintry adulthood,
No change,
Stagnation
And death, death for all adults
Daring to brighten the bleak light;
Emphasizing the essence of revolution.
Hope not to emphasize
For one's head safety?
Thought I of hasty pace
As the clouds sailed over
Moving from West to East
For more than a quarter century;
Yet, the pace, snail's
Only helped the night
That has now met us
At the nick of time,
Hope still knocks at our doors
And we hoped for the break of day,
One to broaden our faces;
But, Hope's real name: Mr. Dixeption
For we never erect the past;
Failures of the past cavy
Must be first, our instructors,
We instead consider garbs
Than cultivate for tomorrow
(Sunning pour powder)
Expecting manna from space
'Cause of this stale word, Hope.
Hope, rebellious Hope!
Inane hamate Hope,
Wicked Hope!
Be good
Be kind
To let us hope for You
Realise success
Spring adulthood
Evolution and progress
And think the world right
Right

Than misconstrue our world
Hopelessly hopefully optimistic.

Machination

They are still bucketing me,
Denucratizing me.
Yesteryears, "an object I was!"
They realized it inhumane,
Left me saying they were humane;
Then went down into History.

Yesteryears, buccaneers here came,
Cross in hand and in cassocks garbed.
"God-sent", they said
To teach, civilize and beg alms
As for these at sea they'd use arms.
The alms they squeezed out
And I cried: Exploitation!
Hurriedly, without mission accomplishment, they left.

For they come back show,
Painters' brush left mine devilish;
Echoing transfer of technology,
One of debt burden
For I sent them no technology
Though not without one.

Today,
Denucratization
Asserts democratization!
I would not this robe
Their very much cherished robe.

The Plebs: Their Chair

The palatial ton load
Behind the nice-to-rock chair groans,
The chair with arms
Though an armchair,
To squatting
And squealing
Arms are the soldiers'
Who are the States'
And the States the Heads'
We will not label Tyrants
Just because they jostle peasants.
The paltry pyramidal organization
Of our spherical portion
Pivots   them;
But we chairs want our Rockers
                                        Unseated.

With their armed arms
Can they rid us
And in vacuum reign?

We See, Only Mourn. *Cities' Debacle.*

tight fisted they stand
arms clutched together
eyes running from head to toe
ready to pounce on each other:
yet, one had dominated;
now is dominated
        coal
        ivory
black is coal
in short evil.
white the voted
     glittering
       ivory
acclaimed,
  now disdained
    for embracing coal's
  materialism
best for big guns health;
spiritual,
      and
          physical
              for wealth
is health
to mat-mongers
suzing and swaggingly
flying to and from hermitage
questing adjustment
of blackened structures
coal started,
         done by the stainless I....
with folded arms
lachrymal eyes
voiceless larynx
all cockerels mourn
for any hiss out would
cost them their breath....
yet, they could be martyrs....

Dragonlike Friday (April Sixth)

On others they it found
Though bullets' grave in him they sought;
For good was he at promises,
Of all, nascent he was.
In the bonnet they him held.

Pope Of Camsima

Adventurers as he in these pranks indulge,
Yesternight was Germany, today Asia, and tomorrow Africa;
Intelligently thou fly the world over.
Bat! Bittering the sugared pills.

Laity thee applaud,
Ulcer of social injustice in scale's name
Addled-brain, this month (November) you brought.
Past glories of the Sahel all gone?

In Our Manger: Are We Strangers?

I shall... I shall if... They've all mastered.
Of all, my voice, my calories. I am robbed.
Know not me for what this be;
The uprightness of the nigrescently painted body...
For, for this paint in the market, light is the purse....
But, if.... Why by my head?
Timorous of disestablishment and from their height slumping...
Why bother, for we are dumb at the call?
No more than a chalet-like silhouette is he,
Our ship's stern brothers lancinate,
Yet, only words.
Turn not our Heads.
How can they? They're their height responsibilities.
As we, agape, to the fields or streets take,
Behind us are hounds sent,
We on frigid floors slump, shackled.
Would we grubby dung carriers others' clean (save)?
The African sage bumpkin unity proposed,
Our Heads they told, "stay divided and stand."
Just what the 1700s them saw.
The sage, hoodlum termed, the first home sent,
Manly African Nationalist Denied Every Legal   Amenities
Himself in obscurity finds,
To hibernation, gone are his colleagues.
Yet, his goblin would and our ship will respire.

The Private

Dull and bleak morn
Promises day's finesse
As I gasped still,
A churl in green to me got.
He fluttered: "gooooodmonin."
As brows make way for the lens
His leafy leaflike garb stunned me.
Still, still….
"Willy" he fluttered again.
Just too many of 'em:
The poet, the teacher,
The steward or the lecher?
For my question
A slap is born on the wall
As my twig respects the wind.
The lesson is across the rift
For a veteran's to touch.

Our House

The House we build at polls
In, meet uncle's comrades
To prattle on our lot,
But their empty upstairs
The claques' nodding perform.

Ours must not be uncle's.
Grandee's script them divide,
Dividing his parlour
From our House depending
For subsistence on his.
Now, our House should stand,
On its pillars standing.

Our House, the builders gilded.
Father's father being lamb
Accepted the grave grange
But, let fall his bread crumbs
Our House with ease enjoyed….
In grandee's, seating today
Our uncle, grandee's first
And would not drop down any
But tiger-like preying.

Nor father nor any
Uncle's action embrace;
The compound deserts him;
Abandoning our House, not erecting another
Nor sending us back home
Creating flowery gardens
In which we shall stand home
But like a dumb he escaped….

For father's father dumb-like escape
Beguiled we stand agape,
Sinking in swamps' forest.
Our fertile village land
Needs a hitch and courage
And there we'll bask ourselves
Like playing eagles at dawn
'planing across the sky in the morning sun.
With backs on walls, we must
To the last wan, wailing, fight.
A stand our House will have

Our fields we'll enclose
Not in this slump gilded house!

Sheepish were father and four uncles
Giving theirs and ours: voices,
Not to this swamps' forest,
To two: grandee's home north
And uncle Ernest's sunset.
Parents were, children, no!
With celerity stand
Them facing their village
Ready for abrogation
Of the oneness unsigned
Nor will it ever be.

Father soloist departs
Not unveiling the mind
Nor with us chanting,
Dreading he becomes one;
Slave to unveiled secret.
The baggage on our head,
Challenge, unburden it
Stand airy in our House,
A House he'd never lease!

Dredging Mokolo Market

Extinguishers never their job did
Yesterday STAMATIADES I watched
To ashes go down
Yet, we had extinguishers
A week after, they could
On market ants, their job do
And under their weight shivered Mokolo.
Yes, right they might have been
For the sake of market "development",
But, the miteless…!
Top on their agenda, malnutrition,
At school doors knocks September
With school requirements yearned.
Yet, mothers' cocoyams crushed,
Our boxes they crushed.
Under the canopy of uniform
Peacemakers, millions
Swashbucklingly took,
And to keep us off, water, they sprayed.
The Lilliputian General Gaston I saw,
Up he went, down he came
In that way to be in the dark read,
While at gun war brink
He does nothing but shrink
Now sending his boys at us
He swaggers away
After ordering itchy water on us
For us to go body scratching.
Why not order their job
Using water to fight fire
Than use her on market ants
Crushing with bulldozer their merchandise?
Yet, we nurse hopes for global health,
Extermination of poverty, malnutrition….

Assassinating Democracy (Insurgence)

Place: Bamenda
Day: 26th of may
Year: 1990
And six of ours
Went down!
Standing their grounds
And for their convictions
And gunned down
By the forces of regression.
I know not what official History say of them!
But, May, the month we screamed out
"Mayday!"
In quest for liberation from the chains of tyranny
Deserves that attention worthy of any Victory.

Martyrs are these six
In this nation where no dead is a hero
For what we live for is the here and now
A less conducive one for a penman!
Yet, I long for that day this Mayday
Shall itself fit into our official commemorations!
Our Martyrs' Mayday
Victory over dictacracy!

Progress

Born,
To adulthood one grows,
A mystery unexplained.
Yet, as children
Obey
Parents
Who misconstruing them

Ripe,
At their demand

Did extricate the overgrown
Unable to pivot their burden
But, would crave worldwide
Glimmer.

The Beggar

Born of the head of this ship
Not without father nor mother,
With land and house ownership
Yet, hands must stretch I;
Even provided for, by day, daily bread.
Content, without them, stretched I not.

Emerging Christlike from the horizon,
Of this mermaid lustre knew not I.
This chameleonized love took I,
On not in me everything's theirs. Mission?
"Turn not to avenge." Said them then.
Prostrated I for it was the Gospel !

My ship I see sinking
My Head, theirs in my colour
Join him them for gravity attraction
And I turn, than with my brothers chat,
Action send them man after man
As I see palanquins march one before another.

Catalysed Generosity,
Of prospective lucre filled,
Embeds their Luciferian coast
I embraced at my cost....

Caught

Dreadful virgin forest webs East,
The winding tuft of ranges North,
West is the blinding twilight
Down South the inundating river
Our forefathers
All man after the other
With heavy hearts did cross,
And through which we must stagger pass
As we wade
For, unturned
Not shall a grain
                    Remain
Just like a dream
When we are green
Dustlike become
Averting parents' glare;
But of life and nothing
                    Thinking
As the sun fades out
Wishing Paradise
Our soul's sole domicile
Though spotted
Hailed by laity
For recompense
And just no thought
None for the gory ignorant
For it is the unique cure
To enclosing a sinecure
As we demand charity
They blink generosity
Against applause,
Forgotten, may be, the cause
Till the last day
We'll for all pay....

Madam Landlord

Fast approaching the twentieth century,
Under the moon walked she
From East to West
And none did she find….
The tropics must she try.
Stood I claiming the tropics
But with Bacchus the overture in me working,
Before cogitating, in she guided me.
In my chalet, she left me
This my dawn that was my hope.
Of the land I owned,
I thought she did to me capitulate
Though neither she nor I did stipulate.
Under an umbrella I see her;
She came!
Sucked empty the core!
Now coming to stare
At the brink of collapse,
That of the structure she left me,
And to force the House together erect
For rats must to their burrows keep
And acclaim out
The dog in lion's she left them
Sending them home through theirs.
That is the way she traps rats.

Viper

The finest complexion
Has he. In the finest silk
Clad, with bile meal system,
Tar filled, with thought bucket
To gulp and belly fill
He claims he is the prefix.
Without awe, we watch him agape.
Venomously, he curls his way through.
And that after cleaning his food tract
And leaving its products for us to clean
Smirking at our moistless-air-efforts to bucket him
Which with great venom imbues his ma... jes... ty....

Legless

History knows them.
Who chopped them?
History?
The sunny south
Lie today....
Crippled and discarded
Rag of time
Waste over loaded
With one sole memory;
The gone good old days.
This lachrymal season
Eyes no reason
For they offered legs
For kegs
To beg,
Tugged to falling back
In the fifty's filthy bag
With a crackle of laughter
Running in from the West,
They caught a cold
For gone is the gold
Weighting strength;
They are legless....
None but father of lower heavens
Could dare such....
Praising a sane, his sloth,
For he desired him down
Yet, all shall go down
In history and the grave
Even the grave!

Soccer Queen

Lying
Thirsty, paper
Beacons pen
Through libidinous
Grey matter
To come grace
Her; desiringly, he
To flow, rushes....
Like desert sand,
Paper gobbles him,
Swelling smooth as would
Well nourished kids;
And he falls off lean,
Incarnating
That with nothing
Of him, but his liquid....
Generous paper
All takes....
Would not on nip shrink
Lose a jot of rain
Though the drain
Herself, Snowy
She holds fast to
Enticing string,
Appealing
Even for numb nips
For it is now history
And he the sapped tree
Void of leaves
Survives....

Spaying South

Beauty, she was beautiful.
Away stolen, wishful-
Ly, when McChine's inception
Was the other side of reality,
An offshore reality
For shipless sheep
Yet to dream Archimedes.
At machine's conception,
She, the beauty,
A polluting sewage,
Was but one out of a trash can,
Humanist Wilberforce, William,
Lauded though,
With more spates
Name no spades!
From behind hurrying
For the Belle's grave digging
Rewarding South
As their bell tolled
To marooning
Her eroded.
Her offspring's backs
Horsewhips'
Steady landing
Chronicles know them
Not more than horses
Hired gratis
From the Tropics
For Tropics
Of the cosmos newly found....
Today's desire,
See them down the mire,
Give arms
To those needing alms
And give a pull downwards
To projecting her outstanding
Out of her tepee standing;
The monument standing
Images remain, spayed,
South paid....
Speechlessly smiles
Embracing fate that piles
Waiting Wagoner rises
And once more drifts....

Her silence lightning's….
Smile, broadened.

Indigentia

Our heads
      Mightily
         Rich   materially
With   earthly   wealth
Warrant millions poor   health
Teeming   in   the   heads' heads,
The erection of their indigence
Over the   heads of indigents' :
A concrete roof
On walls no hoof
Can breakdown;
Their way to drag down
And inter thoughts
And disfigure their import
              By having the world see the colourful palls
               On their discarded galls:
                  Their vice
             For which everyday
             Indigents pay
              The price
           Inside these cold walls
      Yet, satisfying none of those   lulls
           As the indifferent
         Outside would they give it vent!

IUD

On explosion
God's crowded plantation
Squats, sending us need
To rid weed
Leaving Wheat
Neat;
Discard archeologists' silly
Cradle of Lucy:
The grime
With a crime,
Its pigment.
Ridding him, insufficient,
With AIDS transfer,
And since depletion was no worker,
IUD is voted best herbicide
Sending them off sight
Till
They're still
To languishing….
They're minority,
Misery
Piled up stone
With no scone
Nor tea
To bait Mr. Wrunger
Giving them hunger;
And to these plants stressing
Forgiving and loving
Directing these to his pet
Not to the withering weed
Hanging on the street
It is no liver
Just a condoning lover.
After resistance,
Shall ye concur this new stance?

The Ivorian

The pearl quits a perch
For a trench
To heartily fall in trance
Penetrating Ivorian's entrance
Hovered his feet
Under this feat
Enquiring men's feast
When the absence of yeast
Sings present, echoing
Clement nature's no meaning,
She's Clementine,
You in her, she dines
From your reservoir, marooning you
To oblivion sending lure she showed you,
With charmer words you hailed
Now her ivory garb hailstone rain.
Summing done,
With surface
And core together brought to face,
Retina supplied....
Ah! She's Ivorian,
One for Dorian!

The Best Priest

At first, for a mascot took 'em him.
But, finally a rash guy proves he.
For, to be kind hearted and charitable,
He organizes pogroms.
"This be the best sample."
Can one not say this be the best example ever?
For, in sooth, the furrow is
To the mattress that which the mitre is to the field.
The best priest, interfere him not
Ton retort the Tropical Brown Monkeys
But term him and his lackeys
The equatorial forest tortoises and foxes
Caitiffs, fools and devils.
Yet, this be out of the old devil's
Brown is black; they are black.

Gorji *Guano*

Draped was the sun's face,
His glimpse of it vibrated his larynx
His pen embraced the paper we yearned
And the flesh of the leafy castle this tore:
Our head's. he then his shackles commanded
As that of Lilliput for Gulliver's.
His hounds crooked their knees,
Behind BARS lashed
Him, though one, called at this Association.
Thermis' cadaver met he there
To respire thanks to her reproaches,
Queen of the Isles, thank U! Gorji
I now know the inner colour of the sun's face.

The Real Guano

Dropped always by a Grassfield bird;
This one like Gorji
Stood up voicing
Strangeness: Pluralism!
Which needed blood bath
And six hurried to the park and went off.
So it came!
Retarder now claims
To be the promoter,
Relinquishing guano
And barring him from lying on the farm.
But one thing shines like the sun.
He emerged like a stubborn
Stunted oak tree in a storm
Tenaciously negating fall
Chant: "Non Idiots
Join Our Hands Now
For resourceful Unison
Not Discouraging Intellectualism."

A thing abhorred by the prince
Never heeding our cry
But seeking reconciliation
For a crime unknown!
Guano is the only fertilizer
For you plants…!

The Deal: Tough Times

By the board, with jays in front,
In hand a piece of chalk,
He with this, his saliva without ennui exalted,
Beckoned by the dung filled porcelainly shelled egg,
He hankered it for it would his insignia better;
Yet, with his fence repairs by hedging,
At its apex could not retort it.
Finding himself hoe in hand;
Recruit of that which is never unwilling,
No matter from whom comes the application,
Not as those wanting godfathers reject,
To accept,
He like a tortoise in his shell, at mission
Derailment, finds a hideout.

From Then To Date

At three
I remember,
My eyes hosted refugees
Galloping from neighbouring
Nigeria into the Cameroons
Like cows from a thunder stricken herd.
Their hooves sang like the locomotive
Killing me with fright
By night
Dreaming of embracing monsters
To hook on my mother's
Chest.
Dissipating my fears, Parents
In my ears whispered:
"They are plagued by an ill."
The horses did confirm.
I grew up, of the war I read,
My ears drank a myriad saga about same wave,
Jostling me to pondering the devil
Brain mother of that evil
And my gun triggered,
Aimed Western arm merchants
Goading Biafra's slaughter
And burial
In Nigeria
As canapé to economic prowess
Now questing power-tricks
To push one Nigeria
Into many Nigeria
With an umbrella of oneness
"Southerners we are."

Zoorhs

One glimpse around, varying acts;
Money transfer.
Everybody digs their way out of this swarm.
The leaders in this crowd hawk,
Swap from hand to hand,
And no spec of them is seen,
Duped flabbergasted,
In agony dare not shout out.
If they do, to bury the hatchet,
The exalted hawks lull'em.
The digging goes on, footprints left....
Why can't our watch dogs take them in the act?
Goats graze as far as the tether can go.
Great prints leave'em when shackled;
With bones smelling around, our dogs hunt not.
Oiled are their lips. Why bother them?

Coins and Sheets

Smiling devils amongst men
Ununderstood we seem by them.
About us thieves, merchants.... Confabulate
But carrying us along, they
Stand quarrelling.
From a deep slumber we've awaken.
One divorced us after
Making us his prisoners for more than a score.
How grumpy is he a month after?
Take him up the muzzle
Against the meticulous Shah who debauching his insignia
With us for the meantime peters the insurrection.
Neither ignition nor burial would be possible without   us
Accepting us
He turns around to trash all claims
As though he were no mercenary
But a good J...
Need he to embrace us
Manufacture lies and loot us
From the labour of the plebs?
Though we're devils, we cure mahoganic hands
Just as we avert lettuce-like hands
Causing jollity
And not forgetting stolidity.

Mean Idiot

Sensuality is animal.
Killing likewise
Not burying its inhumanity....
And all the bastards,
The gulf massacres,
Name such
Architectural designs
Not of this inferior cast
But, the Almighty's image
The sage
Whose only five senses
Least match any one of animal's six
And none think evolving towards them
But degenerating into them.

Why not think them yourself?

Blacks and the Reds robbed....
Acme of inhumanity...
The act, animals' too?

The mean idiots' !

Chiefdom

In latrine
Through flies doctrine
To larvae
Questing mutism
In the mess
Thrives democracy…!
For able dribblers
Of others
Shall be them
As the sun its roost finds
Kicking History's essence
Like the Early man with none before.

Shark's Shack

Scarecrow built,
Through her glass walls
Just eyes
On her feast.
In aqueous liquor
As in her habitat,
Her majestic swim
Tells eyes
Of glass walls' hooks.
With all the marshals
Circumventing, outside, fishing;
Shark shielding;
To turn after her in draughts
As bait, drumming "tum tum
Tara-ta-ta tum!
She should embrace in water
The wailing fishes.

Heir

A swim across the sea
Was imperative;
His father's depth embrace
Sunrise replace.

His face brightness,
Robe expansiveness,
Hid his knocked knees
And with chant of glories:
Certificated, he was straight....

Yes, straight that day
Like midday sun ray.
Yet, while walking,
Kicked the villagers off stream.
Miles unend they fell
To carry up their heads, unite
His silhouette and the gibe
And in dolour,
Feast lenses with legs "K"
He must undo gravity
From his standing quay....

Grassfield

A child like little Malcolm,
A fighting soldier
Like general Winter,
A Square like Lincoln's,
Place de la Concorde,
Discordances' legacies,
She is full with grasses
And her walls of fig trees
Sprouting thoughts
For Actions and want
For expensive
Unpensive
Commodity:
LIBERTY
On her hill summit
Market
For offspring of her trees
Ripe on their marks to flee.

Their Yearnings

In the name and for the sake of truth
At poles speakers themselves find
Though for an essay they it join:
Right they must say that they see.
Yet, praises are apexes plight:
Nauseous are these desires.
For not producing the yearn,
In gaol they are protected.

Robbery! Why this robbery?
Give it then ano'er name
Than blanket a profession in a choir,
That of praises;
This noble profession, than join it,
I rather set it west not east....

Looking back, one sees a host of them
Who for the sake of truth
Were like Samson taken
And made to creep like Nebuchadnezzar
Under the weight of the shackles;
Those imposed by our bigmen;
Under strain to shape 'cracy
With free larynx vibration.
Yet, when it is time
They heat up the atmosphere
Polluting it
For they are stooges
And would not want the overseers;
Those responsible for their elevation,
To cripple their "Demotic Stands."

Gunner Gone

The eyes that see
Will not across the sea
For once there
There is no way to hear;
Blindness reigns,
And on this side, eyes rain
Even when he that is gone
May have crushed with a gun
The innocent souls
Planted and crushed with soles
To make a new ridge
For he's gone across the bridge.

The Head

Many, at the top of his voice,
The old boa lulls.
Westwardly they behind him turn and line
For uses him nothing but the saints' verses;
Under his heart is the arctic end of heart.
O, know not them; No for Yes would be YES.
Yet, hearts' scribe marches forward and go
How can they negate their NO?

Face not them the goblin to back man,
In this haven
It is q question of making a river flow back to source
Laity must with heads their apostles make
The sheepishness of the ancient bred sighs,
Threw them into hurdles and scuffles;
Horns logging from morn till eve; I watched 'em
Harvest the fruits of their leaders' preaching.

The Village Mountain

A huge monster,
Barren land he towers
Like an emir over his
When land screeches
Out on his marks
He echoes back
'cos he and man on soil rely
on soil he stands, sly,
on soil subsists man
and on man rejoices land
to complete the triangle.

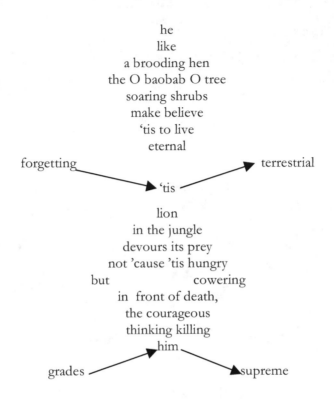

he
like
a brooding hen
the O baobab O tree
soaring shrubs
make believe
'tis to live
eternal

forgetting   terrestrial

'tis

lion
in the jungle
devours its prey
not 'cause 'tis hungry
but   cowering
in front of death,
the courageous
thinking killing
him

grades   supreme

The world a classroom.
I'm   a   teacher
My   name   Am'riquor
Who-is-sane   a   student
So   intelligent
That   to   supersede
In Bushes' almighty me,
Goes in for my practice,
Not only my theories....
Would   sad   arm
Sat   down
Like   others
From   me
Taking orders
For me
To
Glitter
The better
'Cause as a teacher
I'm always right.

as it was
(epilogue)

the king was young
like any other youth
his subjects
could not but vision
a heavenly kingdom
as they viewed glittering his
complexion and meekness
the real portrait of youths
who when aged become dreaded
by folks and subjects
for not even a lion would stand
to face the wrinkles sown by time
when gullies
rifts and valleys
of the face recollect
oozed water from pores sweat's
they shrink
for no want of the grubby
man transformer into dust
for people like drinking water
not drowning in water
if the river is a king
drowning all fishes like a king
owning all the villagers and
even their own land
wounded biles
and nerves
went miles
all frowned
at the crown
inflating laughter
that exploded as a daughter
with ears and eyes
backing the father's advice.

Extricated, Yet On The Fence

O, what a magnificent country
In a thorny calyx thrust! Could it rotate?
Never shouldered were days promises.
It tears us all; the sun's blade.
Yet, screened is our part.
Has it stooges for heads;
Jugglers and card master minders.
But we care not turning, East their heads.
Extricated some five revolutions before I came
In town epicure remains their desire.
Not to one tune I see them dancing;
Gossips, whores, human hunters and hypocrites....
I see it on the fence this day. Dismal ability
To turn theirs East, they turn ours West.
Where are we? Home or out there?
Captured is our phenotype
Not genotype!
Turn then heads East and be Home,
Letting not the ill-baked mosquito in your earphone....

Pastor President

Enchanted is everybody eyeing him. But,
Than drink with the laity,
He widens torments' huts:
"For your benevolence I this do." Says he.
An audacious (k) night
In daylight
Knows in sooth the rope;
The cross must rest in the court.
And to the deplored laity, no rein given.
Yet, under the cross he buckets them,
Figuring them simpletons.
The field their only choice,
In, rush them pouncing like lions
About to kiss the skies....

The Downtrodden

To the street, take me,
Abandoned by them;
This and these be good treatment of me:
With kicks, tossing me around them and spitting on me,
Nature's helping hand extended;
Insane, host I a host of pest.
They will never be thus treated!
Spend I frosty nights to pest
Exposed. Each of them I carry.
But, none of my good hills can,
Amongst them none can all these marry:
Feed me upon the dump filth not pan,
But, wade me not the Nun before any of them.
Why this? Nature, let me them their world.
(To my good oppressors, to them, to them….)
I plea thee screen my sun to brighten their world.

Equality

Like twins, identical,
This chant's ecclesiastical;
For to lull the under-looked,
Having him hooked,
Just one praise
And the rest disgrace
With smiles
Swimming on files
To inter ignominy of this act;
Parallel Paul's Act.
Mortal

                               Petal

Of earth's Flowers
Yearning followers
To stretch hands
As teacher on pulpit stands
With traditional wisdom
Impervious to exotism in his kingdom
Though, so ardent a preacher
Of equality, this teacher!